CW00346973

Content

Tajine of Lamb

Ingredients

Preparation: 30 min Cooking: 1 h

- 2 pieces of saddle of lamb or tender pieces of boneless
- 4 potatoes
- 1/2 zucchini
- 1 tomato
- 1 carrot
- 1 onion
- Green olive
- 1/2 glass of virgin olive oil
- Cumin
- spices (including nutmeg, ginger, coriander, cinnamon ...)
- Yellow saffron (for coloring)
- Pepper
- Salt
- 1/2 glass of water

Step 1

Pour 3/4 tablespoon of oil in the tagine dish directly on the heat or the baking sheet.

2nd step

When the oil is hot, brown the meat on each side (about 10 min).

Stage 3

Lower the heat a little and place the vegetables, washed and roughly cut, in a pyramid over the meat, from the firmest to the most tender (potatoes, then carrot , then zucchini , then onions), interspersed with cumin, 14 spices , salt and pepper.

Step 4

Drizzle with a little water, sprinkle with yellow saffron , to give color and place the green olives.

Step 5

Cover and cook over low heat for 30 minutes.

Step 6

At the end of this time, place on the cooked vegetables, the tomatoes cut into pieces, cover and cook for another 15 minutes.

Step 7

Serve hot, directly on the table, with tea and unleavened bread .

Veal Tagine

Ingredients

Preparation: 30 min Cooking: 1 h

- 1 kg of veal in pieces (hock or shoulder type)
- 1 onion (or 2 small)
- 1 crushed tomato (or a few crushed canned tomatoes or even a little tomato coulis with water)
- 1 teaspoon of ginger
- 1 teaspoon paprika
- 2 bouillon cubes
- 1 bay leaf
- 5 saffron (optional but a plus for the dish)
- 2 cloves of chopped garlic
- 1 tablespoon chopped parsley (even freeze-dried)

Step 1

In a tagine dish (failing this, in a Dutch oven with a lid having a small hole), put the meat and sprinkle with salt, pepper, the diluted cubes, ginger , paprika , saffron, garlic , parsley and place the bay leaf. Drizzle with oil (we are not a tablespoon closer!) And mix to impregnate the meat.

2nd step

Put the dish on the heat and let it cook until the pieces are golden. Meanwhile, peel the onion, tomato and the vegetables you have chosen. When the pieces of meat are golden brown, arrange them as best as possible in the dish as they will not move.

Stage 3

Then mince the onion (even two if you like) and spread it over the meat. Do the same with the tomato.

Step 4

Divide the vegetables by stacking them knowing that the longest to cook should always be at the bottom (carrots for example) and the most fragile at the top (cauliflower). Once everything is superimposed, nothing is touched.

- 2 spoons of olive oil (otherwise argan or sunflower)
- Pepper to your taste
- Salt
- Carrot
- Cauliflower

Step 5

Add a small glass of water to the side of the dish, not directly on the food impregnated with spices and decorate with freshly ground pepper or paprika or parsley sprinkled on the vegetables above.

Step 6

Cook until the water reduces and forms a sauce (about 1 hour 30 minutes over low heat). Half-open the lid at the end of cooking to help reduce the sauce.

Step 7

Attention, it may be necessary to add water during cooking so watch from time to time.

Step 8

Serve with bread because traditional tagine is not used with semolina!

Step 9

Good tasting.

Lamb tagine with honey and onions

Ingredients

Preparation: 30 min Cooking: 1 h

- 1 kg of lamb (collar, boneless rib ...)
- 500 g baby onions
- 100 g liquid honey
- 1 teaspoon of ginger powder
- 1 cinnamon stick
- 1 pinch of saffron filaments
- 2 spoons of olive oil
- 1 handful of hulled almonds (optional)
- 2 handfuls of raisins (optional)
- Pepper
- Salt

Step 1

Cut the meat into large cubes. Peel the baby onions (soak them in a bowl of cold water 20 minutes before to peel them more easily).

2nd step

Heat the oil in a baking dish or casserole dish in the oven and on the fire. Brown the pieces of meat with 2 onions.

Stage 3

Add the grapes if you have any, honey, ginger , cinnamon and saffron . Salt and pepper.

Step 4

Stir and cover with water. Cover and simmer for about 1 hour over low heat.

Step 5

Remove the meat and set aside.

Step 6

Reduce the cooking juices to three quarters, then put the meat back. Add the remaining onions and cover.

Step 7

Slide into the oven at 200 ° C (thermostat 6-7) and cook for 45 min.

Step 8

Just before serving, sprinkle with dry roasted almonds. Serve with couscous or potato semolina (which can be added to the dish before baking).

Chicken tagine

Ingredients

Preparation: 30 min Cooking: 1 h

- 4 chicken thighs
- 2 zucchini
- 3 potatoes
- 2 carrots
- 2 tomatoes
- 1 onion
- tagine spices
- Cumin
- 1 tablespoon olive oil
- Water

Step 1

Brown the chicken over medium heat so that it is a little golden.

2nd step

Meanwhile, peel and cut the vegetables: cut the carrots in half, then lengthwise. Ditto for the zucchini . Cut the onions into strips and the potatoes into 4.

Stage 3

Put the vegetables with the chicken, add the tagine spices and the cumin. Also put a little water (3/4 glass of water).

Step 4

Cook for about 1 hour and that's it, it's ready!

Moroccan chicken tagine

Ingredients

- 4 chicken thighs
- 1 onion , sliced
- 2 cloves of chopped garlic
- 2 tomatoes, peeled , seeded and diced
- 1 teaspoon paprika
- 1 teaspoon 4 spice mix
- 1 teaspoon of cinnamon
- 1 teaspoon of cumin
- 1 teaspoon of saffron
- 1/2 teaspoon ginger
- 1 small can of chickpeas
- 1 boiling water with 2 gold cubes

Preparation: 40 min
Cooking: 45 min

Step 1

In a bowl, mix the spices and the cloves of garlic .

2nd step

In another bowl, mix the diced tomatoes , lemon and honey.

Stage 3

Remove the skin from the chicken and brown in a hot casserole dish with a little olive oil.

Step 4

When the chicken is golden brown, remove it from the casserole dish and replace with the onion (if necessary add a little olive oil).

Step 5

As soon as the onions start to brown, add the chicken thighs, then the spice mixture, the tomato, lemon and honey mixture and drizzle with the broth until the thighs are well covered.

Step 6

Then add the grapes and chickpeas, salt, pepper and possibly add tabasco.

- 1 lemon, peeled and coarsely diced
- 3 tablespoons of honey
- 100 g raisins
- Pepper and a little tabasco
- Salt

Step 7

As soon as it boils, lower the heat and simmer for about 45 minutes. Serve with fine semolina even better.

Step 8

Enjoy your meal.

Monkfish tagine

Ingredients

- 1.5 kg of monkfish tail (ask your fishmonger to cut them into sections)
- 6 tablespoons olive oil
- 4 teaspoons powdered cayenne pepper
- 4 teaspoons ground cumin
- 3 cloves
- Pepper
- Salt
- 1 untreated lemon
- 1 onion

Preparation: 30 min
Cooking: 30 min

Step 1

In a large dish, mix 2 tablespoons of olive oil, chilli, cumin and cloves. Add salt and pepper. Let the monkfish marinate in this mixture for 1 hour, mixing from time to time so that the pieces are well coated with the preparation.

2nd step

Wash the lemon, cut it into slices. Peel and chop the garlic and the onion .

Stage 3

In a Dutch oven, brown the onion, garlic and lemon slices over medium heat, in the rest of the olive oil.

Step 4

Let simmer for 10 minutes, without coloring.

- 3 garlic cloves
- 1 large can of peeled and chopped tomatoes
- 2 good pinches of saffron
- 1 can of pitted black olives (about 200 g)

Step 5

Add the tomatoes , monkfish and the rest of the marinade .

Step 6

Sprinkle with saffron . Cook for 15 minutes.

Step 7

Add the olives and finish cooking for another 5 minutes.

Step 8

Serve immediately with fragrant rice.

Jerusalem artichoke tagine

Ingredients

Preparation: 10 min
Cooking: 35 min

- 1 kg Jerusalem artichoke
- 2 garlic cloves
- 2 onions
- 2 carrots
- Parsley
- 10 cl olive oil
- 12 black olives
- 1 pinch of saffron
- nutmeg
- Pepper
- Salt
- 10 cl hot water

Step 1

Peel the Jerusalem artichokes , rinse them in vinegar water and dry them.

2nd step

Cut them into small pieces.

Stage 3

Peel and mash the garlic.

Step 4

Peel and chop the onions and carrots .

Step 5

Chop the parsley.

Step 6

In the tagine dish (or a casserole dish or wok) brown the garlic and onion in the oil.

Step 7

Add the Jerusalem artichokes and carrots with the olives and parsley.

Step 8

Sprinkle with saffron and nutmeg .

Step 9

Salt and pepper.

Step 10

Pour the hot water.

Step 11

Mix well.

Step 12

Cook for 35 min over low heat.

Jerusalem artichoke tagine

Ingredients

Preparation: 20 min
Cooking: 30 min

- 500 g minced meat, chicken breasts or livers.
- 1 onion
- 4 potatoes
- 1 large handful of parsley
- 12 eggs
- 200 g grated cheese (emmental, gruyère, Comté ...)
- Cumin
- Salt
- Pepper

Step 1

Cut the potatoes into small pieces (size sautéed apple) and fry.

2nd step

Meanwhile, in an oiled pan, brown the selected meat and then the onions .

Stage 3

Once the meat is golden brown, add the sautéed potatoes and a good handful of chopped parsley, cumin, salt and pepper.

Step 4

Cook for 1 min while stirring then allow to cool.

Step 5

In a bowl, beat the eggs with the cheese in an omelet . Add the mixture of meat and potatoes to the bowl and mix.

Step 6

Butter a gratin dish (rectangular) and pour the mixture into it. Bake for about 30 minutes in the oven at 230 ° C (thermostat 7-8).

Step 7

Once your tagine is cooked, take it out of the oven and let it cool for 1 hour before cutting it into small squares of about 5 cm.

Author's note

You can mix your meats very well: livers with chicken breasts ... but also add a few green olives in small pieces to the mixture. Accompany pleasantly a mixed salad or even better a good Tunisian salad.

Couscous-style tagine

Ingredients

- 1 eggplant
- 2 medium zucchini
- 4 medium tomatoes
- 1 red bell pepper
- 1 green pepper
- 1 chili
- 400 g chickpeas (1 box)
- For the seasoning:
- 2 medium onions
- 2 garlic cloves
- Coriander seeds
- Pepper

Preparation: 30 min
Cooking: 6 h

Step 1

Soak the raisins in lukewarm water 1 hour before.

2nd step

Drain them before use.

Stage 3

Wash and cut all your vegetables into pieces.

Step 4

Peel onions and garlic .

Step 5

Roughly chop the onion , cut the garlic into 4.

Step 6

Heat your tagine with olive oil, add the onions, garlic and vegetables (except chickpeas).

Step 7

Spice to taste.

- Cumin
- 100 g raisins
- 3 tablespoons olive oil
- For meats:
- 6 pieces of chicken
- 6 pieces of lamb (stew)
- 6 merguez
- Salt
- Paprika

Step 8

Place the chicken and lamb on top.

Step 9

Spice again.

Step 10

Cook for 3 to 4 hours.

Step 11

Add the merguez.

Step 12

Cook for about 1 hour.

Step 13

Add the chickpeas (they are already cooked).

Step 14

Simmer until ready to serve, lowering the heat if necessary.

Step 15

Serve with semolina prepared separately.

1

Tajine of the fisherman

Ingredients

Preparation: 20 min
Cooking: 40 min

- 2 sea bream (or white fish)
- 3 tomatoes
- olives
- 3 cloves of garlic, crushed
- 2 lemons
- Coriander / chopped parsley
- Salt
- Sweet paprika
- Strong paprika
- Cumin
- Table oil
- Vinegar

Step 1

In a salad bowl, prepare the chermoula: mix the herbs, spices, salt , and garlic .

2nd step

Drizzle with table oil or olive oil.

Stage 3

Add a little vinegar.

Step 4

Mix.

Step 5

In the tagine , place the tomato rings .

Step 6

Coat the fish (the inside and the outside of it).

Step 7

Arrange in the tagine dish, on the tomato rings.

Step 8

Pour the rest of the chermoula over it.

Step 9

Garnish with the slices of tomatoes, lemon, and olives.

Step 10

Sprinkle with strong paprika and a drizzle of table oil.

Step 11

Cover.

Step 12

Cook everything in tagine over charcoal.

Step 13

After cooking, serve.

Tajine créole

Ingredients

- 300 g peeled pink shrimp
- 300 g fresh tuna or monkfish or firm fish
- 300 g mussels or cockles (net)
- 20 spoons of coconut milk
- 2 yellow peppers
- 1 lime
- 300 g green beans or eat everything
- 6 tomatoes
- 2 garlic cloves

Preparation: 30 min
Cooking: 15 min

Step 1

Peel and dice the 2 yellow peppers .

2nd step

Take 1/2 lime zest , and squeeze it to collect the juice.

Stage 3

Peel and seed the tomatoes , dice them.

Step 4

Heat the olive oil in a wok or a frying pan, sear successively the peeled shrimps, then the fish (be careful not to overcook) and remove them from the heat.

Step 5

Sear the peppers, add the lime juice and the 2 chopped garlic cloves. Lower the heat and cook this set for 10 minutes in olive oil.

2 pinches of Espelette pepper

- 2 tablespoons olive oil

Step 6

Open the mussels or cockles in a pan, without letting them cook. Remove the shells.

Step 7

Add the tomatoes, shrimp and fish, cockles or mussels.

Step 8

Season with Espelette pepper and a little salt if necessary.

Author's note

Can prepare in advance. Guaranteed success! Be careful not to overcook shrimp, mussels, cockles, and fish. Leave the peppers to candy a little in the lemon olive oil.

Tajine Of Chicken To Apricots

Ingredients

- 125 g semi-dried apricots
- 4 chicken breasts
- 50 g raisins
- 2 onions
- 2 tablespoons of honey
- 1 teaspoon of cinnamon
- 1 teaspoon of cumin
- handful flaked almonds
- 30 g butter
- 2 tablespoons olive oil
- Pepper

Preparation: 20 min
Cooking: 1 h

Step 1

Melt butter in a pan. Add the onions and reduce them. Reserve the onions.

2nd step

Meanwhile, cut the chicken breasts into pieces (not too small to keep the chicken soft).

Stage 3

Heat the olive oil in a tagine dish . Brown the chicken pieces.

Step 4

Add honey, apricots , cinnamon and cumin. Season with salt and pepper and sprinkle with 20 cl of water. Cover and simmer 45 min.

Step 5

Add the almonds in the tagine with candied onions and grapes dry. Continue cooking 30 min.

Salt

- Coriander (falcutative)

Step 6

Optionally, sprinkle with the chopped cilantro , just before serving.

Author's note

Serve this tagine with semolina. You can replace apricots with mirabelle plums in season.

Five spice tagine

Ingredients

Preparation: 30 min
Cooking: 3 h

- 500 g chicken breast (this tagine can also be made only with vegetables)
- 2 zucchini
- 2 eggplants
- 2 orange red peppers
- 5 carrots
- 3 onions
- 2 garlic cloves
- 100 g dried apricots
- 150 g almonds
- 2 lemons
- Olive oil

Step 1

The recipe is quite easy and is prepared in a large saucepan over medium heat.

2nd step

Lightly brown vegetables and chicken in olive oil.

Stage 3

Let them sweat without browning them: stir for a good 5 minutes to make them work a little!

Step 4

Pour the water, the spices and the juice of the two lemons (you can put the lemon skins in the pan): stir again so that everything is well impregnated.

Step 5

Add the 2 spoons of honey, apricots and almonds (keep ten almonds for decorating the dish).

Five-spice turmeric, cumin seeds, ginger powder (or grated ginger), cinnamon (a stick), nutmeg (a good pinch of each spice)

- 10 cl of water
- Pepper
- Salt
- 2 large tablespoons of honey

Step 6

Simmer gently for 2 to 3 hours.

Step 7

During cooking, you can taste it from time to time to check the tone of the seasoning and correct it with either spice if necessary.

Step 8

Serve with couscous seed .

Rabbit tagine

Ingredients

Preparation: 20 min
Cooking: 1 h

- 1 rabbit in pieces or thighs
- 2 onions
- 2 doses of saffron
- 2 cinnamon sticks
- 3 handfuls of black raisins
- 4 teaspoons of honey
- Cornflour

Step 1

In a casserole dish, brown the meat in olive oil.

2nd step

Add the sliced onions .

Stage 3

Add cinnamon and raisins .

Step 4

Add the saffron diluted in 1/2 glass of water.

Step 5

Cover and simmer 3 / 4h-1h.

Step 6

To make the sauce, remove the rabbit pieces from the casserole dish.

Step 7

In it, put the honey, 1 tablespoon of maizena diluted in a glass of water, and mix.

Step 8

If there is not enough sauce, you can add a glass of water.

Step 9

Return the rabbit, and serve very hot, accompanied by tagliatelle.

Tagine of fish

Ingredients

Preparation: 30 min
Cooking: 40 min

- 400 g mussels
- 3 onions
- 600 g potato
- 1/2 lemon
- 1/2 teaspoon ground ginger , cumin and sweet pepper
- 600 g whiting
- Fresh coriander
- Olive oil
- Pepper
- Salt

Step 1

Clean the molds. Peel and cut the potatoes into rings, wash and cut the lemon into quarters.

2nd step

In a casserole or tajine dish , sweat the chopped onions for 2 min and the spices in 2 tablespoons of oil.

Stage 3

Add the vegetables, 50 cl of water, salt and pepper and bring to the boil. Cook, covered, 15 min over medium heat. Then place the fish fillets and lemon there, continue cooking over low heat, 10 min, covered.

Step 4

Add the mussels, mix, cover and open them over low heat (approx 10 min).

Step 5

Garnish with chopped fresh cilantro , serve.

Salmon tagine

Ingredients

Preparation: 30 min
Cooking: 1 h

- 4 salmon fillets
- 6 potatoes
- 100 g peas
- 2 tablespoons tagine spices
- 1/2 l fish broth
- Sunflower oil
- 1 onion
- Salt
- Pepper

Step 1

Brown the onions in the tagine with the sunflower oil.

2nd step

Cut the potatoes into cubes and then incorporate them with the onions, let sear for 10 minutes.

Stage 3

Then add the peas, spices, salt and pepper .

Step 4

Mix well and then add the fish broth.

Step 5

Put the salmon fillets on the preparation, cover and cook for 1 hour on low heat.

Lamb tagine with dried apricots

Ingredients

Preparation: 20 min
Cooking: 30 min

- 1.2 kg boneless lamb
- 3 onions
- 1 kg carrot
- 18 dried apricots (+ if affinity)
- 4 teaspoons of Ras el Hanout
- 1 tablespoon of honey
- 1 drizzle of olive oil
- Salt
- Coriander, finely chopped for presentation

Step 1

Cut the meat into pieces.

2nd step

Thinly slice the onions.

Stage 3

Peel and cut the carrots into pieces.

Step 4

In a pressure cooker put the meat, the oil fillet, the onions.

Step 5

Mix gently, sprinkle with raz el hanout , remix.

Step 6

Add the apricots , carrots, honey and salt.

Step 7

Mix gently ....

Step 8

Put 2 glasses of water in the casserole dish (300 ml), close and cook for 20 minutes from the whistling of the casserole dish.

Step 9

Serve with semolina (with or without grapes) or bulgur ...

Lamb tagine with dried apricots

Ingredients

- 1.2 kg boneless lamb shoulder
- 2 garlic cloves
- 1 tablespoon ground cumin
- 1 teaspoon of ginger powder
- 1/2 teaspoon sweet pepper powder
- Pepper
- Salt
- Oil
- 2 onions
- Flat parsley
- Fresh coriander
- 12 ripe apricots
- 50 g butter

Preparation: 45 min
Cooking: 1 h

Step 1

Cut the meat into cubes.

2nd step

Chop the garlic and mix with the spices (cumin, ginger , chilli), salt and pepper to taste.

Stage 3

In a tagine , put the meat with the garlic mixture, 4 tablespoons of oil and 1/2 glass of water.

Step 4

Mix everything to coat the meat well. Add coarsely chopped onions, 6 sprigs of parsley and 6 finely chopped fresh coriander .

Step 5

Mix well.

Step 6

Place on low heat by interposing a diffuser.

Granulated
sugar

- 125 g almonds,
  peeled

Step 7

As soon as the sauce begins to bubble, cover with the tapered conical tajine.

Step 8

Cook 45 minutes over low heat.

Step 9

Meanwhile, prepare the apricots , wash them, and pit them.

Step 10

In a frying pan, brown them in butter just to brown them. Sprinkle with sugar and lightly caramelize them.

Step 11

In a skillet, dry brown the almonds.

Step 12

After 45 minutes of cooking, add the apricots and almonds to the tagine.

Step 13

Mix gently and continue cooking for 30 minutes, covered.

Step 14

Serve with white rice or raisin semolina .

Step 15

Enjoy your meal !

Tagine of various vegetables

Ingredients

Preparation: 15 min
Cooking: 25 min

- 2 tomatoes
- 2 turnips
- 700 g potato
- 2 onions
- 2 garlic cloves
- 80 g olives
- 2 tablespoons olive oil
- 15 cl vegetable broth
- 4 sprigs of flat parsley
- 4 sprigs of coriander
- 1 level teaspoon ground cumin
- Pepper
- Salt

Step 1

Immerse the tomatoes in boiling water for a few seconds. Peel, seed and crush them.

2nd step

In a casserole dish, brown the chopped onions with the hot oil. Add the potatoes and the turnips, peeled and diced, the crushed tomatoes, chopped herbs, cumin , chopped garlic, olives and vegetable broth . Lightly salt and pepper.

Stage 3

Cover and cook for 25 minutes. Serve hot.

Author's note

Lightly crush the olives to release more fragrance. Serve as a dish, or as an accompaniment.

Tagine with beans

Ingredients

Preparation: 30 min
Cooking: 2 h

- 4 rabbit saddles
- 4 onions
- 1 kg of fresh beans
- Garlic powder, about 1 teaspoon
- 1/2 lemon
- Cinnamon powder, a good pinch
- Cumin , about 1 teaspoon
- Saffron 2 doses
- Salt
- 1 cube of vegetable broth

Step 1

Mince the onions and brown them in the pan in two tablespoons of olive oil. Remove the onions and put them either in a tagine dish or in a large earthen pie dish .

2nd step

Salt the onions, put the saffron , sprinkle with cinnamon , cumin, put the lemon juice and mix everything well.

Stage 3

Add a tablespoon of olive oil to the pan and put the rabbit saddles to brown. Once golden, place on the bed of onions.

Step 4

Heat 1/2 liter of water and dissolve the vegetable broth in it. Pour over the rabbit. Add the country ham cut into small pieces.

1 slice of country ham (Bayonne or other)

- 3 tablespoons olive oil

Step 5

Cover and put in a thermostat 6 hot oven for 1 hour.

Step 6

Peel the beans, and remove their second skin, add them to the preparation after the first hour of cooking. Put back to cook for 1 hour 30 minutes always at 6 of the thermostat.

Step 7

Serve and enjoy.

Fish tagine with vegetables

Ingredients

- 1 kg of tomato
- 3 green peppers
- 2 branches of basil
- 1 leek
- 3 onions
- 3 garlic cloves
- 1/2 glass of olive oil
- 1/2 teaspoon celery
- 1 teaspoon of turmeric
- 6 saithe
- 1 lemon
- Salt
- 1 teaspoon white pepper

Preparation: 35 min
Cooking: 55 min

Step 1

Cut the tomatoes in 8. Cut the peppers into strips. Coarsely chop the basil . Thinly slice the leeks . Mince the onions and squeeze the garlic.

2nd step

Melt the leek, onions and garlic in the olive oil. Add the tomatoes, peppers, celery , turmeric , basil, pepper and salt.

Stage 3

Mix, cover and simmer for 15 minutes.

Step 4

Cut the steaks into 8, removing the skin and the central edge. Add them to the vegetables. Continue cooking, always on low heat and covered, basting the fish from time to time with the vegetable juice.

Step 5

Pour the lemon juice 5 minutes before removing the fish from the heat.

Tagine of kefta with potatoes and peas

Ingredients

Preparation: 30 min
Cooking: 35 min

- 400 g minced meat (kefta)
- 6 potatoes
- 400 g peas
- 3 onions
- 3 tomatoes
- 1 tablespoon chopped cilantro
- 1/2 glass of melted butter tea + mixed olive oil
- 3 glasses of water tea
- 1/2 tablespoon of food coloring (Arabic grocery stores)

Step 1

In a tagine , pot or wok , brown the onions in the butter + oil mixture for 6 to 8 min, over medium heat.

2nd step

Stir in the peeled and quartered potatoes and the water, and cook for 15 min over high heat.

Stage 3

Meanwhile, in a bowl, mix (by hand) the kefta, spices and soaked bread (drained).

Step 4

Add peas, smen and quartered tomatoes and cook for 5 min, then add the kefta balls and cook over low heat for 8 to 10 min.

1 bouillon cube

- 1/4 tablespoon turmeric
- 1/4 tablespoon pepper
- 1/4 teaspoon Moroccan rancid butter , optional)
- 1 tablespoon sweet paprika
- 1/3 tablespoon ginger
- 1/3 tablespoon cumin
- 1/3 tablespoon cinnamon
- 1/3 tablespoon pepper
- 1 gold kub cube
- 1/2 teaspoon caster sugar

Duck tagine with apricots and plantain

Ingredients

Preparation: 15 min
Cooking: 1h30

- 4 duck legs (with bone)
- 8 apricots
- 2 plantains
- 2 spoons of olive oil
- 1 teaspoon ground cumin
- 1 glass of clear water
- 2 teaspoons chopped fresh coriander (do not chop the coriander because it loses all its aroma and taste)
- 2 fresh mint leaves, finely chopped into strips

Step 1

Very important:

2nd step

This recipe is prepared in a real tagine . A tagine is a baking dish in glazed terracotta, from the Middle East countries and can be purchased in stores specializing in Magreb products, for a low price (around 20 euros for a medium-sized tagine).

Stage 3

It can be used on all types of cooking fire and can be put in the oven.

Step 4

Preparation:

Step 5

Boil the plantains for 3 min in clear water to facilitate their peeling.

Step 6

Peel the plantains and cut them into 3 to 4 cm thick pieces.

- Pepper mill
- Salt

Step 7

Put the tagine on low heat, pour the olive oil and half a glass of clear water. Add the bananas.

Step 8

Remove the larger fat parts from the duck legs .

Step 9

After 20 minutes of cooking the bananas add the duck legs in the tagine.

Step 10

Sprinkle with the cumin powder, salt and pepper to taste.

Step 11

Cook over low heat for 15 min.

Step 12

Pit and cut the apricots into quarters, add them to the tagine with a little half glass of water.

Step 13

Simmer for 45 minutes without stirring and ensuring that there is always a cooking juices at the bottom of the tagine.

Step 14

This dish is ready to be eaten when the duck meat starts to come off the bone and when you plant a knife blade in the bananas, it sinks like a baked potato .

Step 15

Before serving, sprinkle your dish with coriander and mint, chopped into strips

Step 16

Serve this dish very hot.

Chicken tagine with dried apricots and raisins

Ingredients

Preparation: 20 min
Cooking: 2h30

- 5 chicken thighs (or a cut chicken)
- 1 untreated lemon
- 5 coriander leaves
- 40 cl of fat - free chicken stock
- 1 good handful of blond grapes
- 1 good handful of dried apricots (100 to 150 g depending on taste)
- 3 medium-sized onions (or one large and two small)

Step 1

Cooking: 2h30 to consume immediately (or 2h the day before then 30 min the next day).

2nd step

Start by soaking the apricots and the grapes in lukewarm water to make them swell.

Stage 3

Then lightly brown the chicken in a little oil in a casserole dish, it should be barely cooked.

Step 4

Pepper and salt the meat.

Step 5

In a frying pan, brown the onions in a little oil, then add them to the casserole dish.

1 fresh ginger

- Salt
- Pepper
- Cooking oil

Step 6

Add the chopped ginger (or finely chopped), the chopped cilantro and the lemon cut into thin slices (it may seem like a whole lemon, but it depends on the amount of apricots and grapes that the If you put a lot like me it is better to put a whole lemon to enhance the taste).

Step 7

Pour the chicken stock all over , the chicken must be submerged (but not submerged!).

Step 8

Cover, then cook over very low heat ("1" for an electric hob) for 1h30-2h so that the chicken is very tender.

Step 9

The next day, cook 20/30 min over medium heat (3 on the hot plate) before serving.

Step 10

It is also possible to cook it at once to serve it the same evening, but it's better the next day!

Step 11

Enjoy your meal.

Tagine yum yum chicken, candied lemons and cherry tomatoes

Ingredients

Preparation: 10 min
Cooking: 1 h

- 1.4 kg of chicken thigh (replaceable with other pieces)
- 3 good handfuls of cherry tomatoes
- 3 candied lemons (mine is very small so it depends on taste)
- 2 onions
- 3 garlic cloves
- 1 tablespoon of tomato puree
- 1 tablespoon ginger (fresh or frozen)

Step 1

Brown the chicken well in the olive oil. Add the minced onions, chopped garlic, spices (ginger , cinnamon , celery salt), pepper and cover with water.

2nd step

Simmer over low heat and covered 35 min.

Stage 3

Add the cherry tomatoes , the tomato puree (relaxed with a little cooking broth) and the preserved lemons cut into large pieces (or chopped if you don't like to eat them during tasting).

Step 4

Let simmer again 40 min half covered (but there we can not be astride over time, the sauce has thickened and must be short).

- 1 tablespoon cinnamon powder
- 1 tablespoon celery salt (optional)
- Olive oil
- Pepper
- Salt

Step 5

Taste and salt if necessary only now, because the lemons are already salted.

Tomato and cilantro meatball tagine

Ingredients

Preparation: 30 min
Cooking: 50 min

- 4 onions
- Olive oil
- 1 kg of peeled tomatoes or tomato pulp (canned)
- 1 small can of tomato puree
- 2 potatoes
- 1 cube of beef broth
- 800 g minced beef
- 4 slices of sandwich bread
- 2 garlic cloves
- 4 eggs
- Thyme
- Parsley and coriander

Step 1

1) prepare the sauce: in the casserole, brown 2 onions without coloring in the olive oil then add the peeled tomatoes, concentrate, the broth, the thyme, salt and pepper. Simmer for 20 minutes, covered.

2nd step

2) cook the potatoes .

Stage 3

Meanwhile, slightly wet the bread , peel and mince the garlic + 2 onions.

Step 4

3) peel and mash the potatoes.

Step 5

4) knead the crumb + the meat + minced onions + garlic + potatoes. Add the beaten eggs + chopped parsley and coriander to the mince . Mix then salt and pepper.

Step 6

5) make large meatballs (about 20), pass them in the flour and cook them in a frying pan. Once golden, gently place them on the tomato sauce and continue cooking over low heat for 20 minutes.

Step 7

6) Serve hot with the rest of chopped cilantro for decoration.

Chicken tagine with pumpkin and dried fruit

Ingredients

Preparation: 10 min
Cooking: 1 h

- 2 tablespoons olive oil
- 1 chicken cut into pieces or thighs
- 12 dried apricots
- 6 prunes
- 2 tablespoons flaked almonds
- 2 tablespoons of raisins
- 2 garlic cloves
- 1 tablespoon turmeric
- 1 cinnamon stick
- 500 g pumpkin, cut into pieces
- Parsley & Coriander & Water

Step 1

Heat the olive oil.

2nd step

Brown the chicken or thighs, garlic and almonds.

Stage 3

Powder turmeric .

Step 4

Let brown 5 min.

Step 5

Add the apricots , grapes, prunes and cinnamon stick .

Step 6

Cover with pumpkin pieces .

Step 7

Add the water and simmer for 1 hour minimum over low heat.

Step 8

Serve with parsley and cilantro .

Turkey Tagine with Grapes and Onions

Ingredients

Preparation: 40 min
Cooking: 30 min

- 6 turkey cutlets
- 200 g raisins
- 1 kg of onion
- 6 tablespoons of orange blossom
- 1 garlic clove
- 5 tablespoons rapeseed oil
- 1/5 g saffron
- 1 bunch of parsley
- 3 teaspoons of cinnamon
- 1 tablespoon of honey
- 1/2 teaspoon ginger
- 3 teaspoons of brown sugar

Step 1

In a bowl, soak the raisins in the orange blossom diluted in 20 cl of water for 1 hour.

2nd step

Make small incisions in the turkey cutlets. Rub them with garlic then keep them cool.

Stage 3

Cut the onions (except one) into strips. Put them in a Dutch oven with 2 tablespoons of rapeseed oil. Let them sweat for a few minutes, stirring them from time to time.

Step 4

Add the brown sugar, 2 teaspoons of cinnamon , the raisins and leave to simmer for 20 min.

Step 5

In a pressure cooker (if you did not have a tagine), brown the onion that remains with 3 tablespoons of rapeseed oil.

Step 6

Add salt and pepper. Add the saffron , ginger , 1 teaspoon of cinnamon, parsley and simmer.

Step 7

Place the turkey cutlets in this same dish, adding 20 cl of lukewarm water. Cover and cook for ten minutes.

Step 8

When they are cooked add the honey, add the preparation based on grapes and onions. Simmer over very low heat for about ten minutes.

Printed in Great Britain
by Amazon